D1737091

THE
OPOSSUM

BY
EMILY CROFFORD

EDITED BY
JULIE BACH

New York

LIBRARY OF CONGRESS CATALOGING IN PUBLICATION DATA

Crofford, Emily.
    The opossum

    (Wildlife, habits & habitat)
    Includes index.
    SUMMARY: Examines the physical characteristics, behavior, and natural environment of the common opossum.
    1. Virginia opossum—Juvenile literature.   2. Opossums—Juvenile literature.
    [1. Opossums.]   I. Title.   II. Series.
    QL737.M34C76   1990   4599.2—dc20   89-28269
    ISBN 0-89686-518-5

PHOTO CREDITS:

Cover: Photo Researchers: (Pat & Tom Leeson)
Photo Researchers: (Jeff Lepore) 4, 17, 19, 22, 35; (Pat & Tom Leeson) 9, 10; (Leonard Lee Rue) 15, 32; (Patricia Caulfield) 21; (Karl H. Maslowski) 24; (Ken M. Highfill) 28, 31; (Will McIntyre) 36; (John J. Dommers) 39; (Jany Salivanet) 42-43
DRK Photo: (Wayne Lynch) 12, 26, 27; (Stephen J. Krasemann) 33

CRESTWOOD HOUSE

Macmillan Publishing Company
866 Third Avenue
New York, NY 10022
Collier Macmillan Canada, Inc.

Printed in the United States of America
First Edition
10 9 8 7 6 5 4 3 2 1

TABLE OF CONTENTS

INTRODUCTION:

The sun slips below the horizon. Dusk gathers in the quiet woods. A mother opossum comes out of her nest and begins her nightly search for food. She needs a lot of nourishment to keep her milk flowing to the babies she carries in her pouch.

The opossum has always fascinated people. The prehistoric Hopewells made pipes in the shape of an opossum some 2,500 years ago. The Chickasaws carved opossum images on water bottles. The Seminoles sang a sad song about a mother opossum and her lost baby. People still tell stories about opossums. The town of Arcadia, Louisiana, even has an annual Possum Festival.

An opossum begins its nightly search for food.

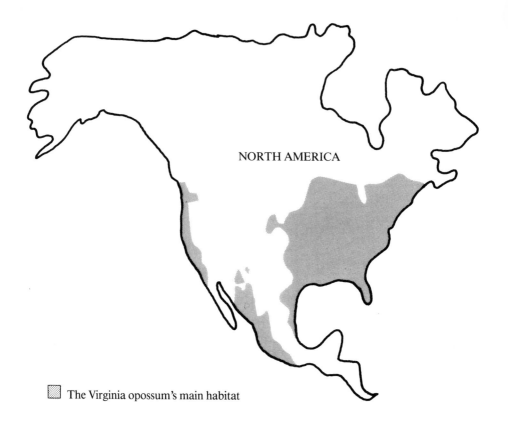

NORTH AMERICA

The Virginia opossum's main habitat

CHAPTER ONE:

The scientific name for the common, or Virginia, opossum is *Didelphis virginiana*. It is a *marsupial*, an animal that generally carries its underdeveloped young in a pouch. Some marsupials do not have pouches, but only folds of skin around the nipples. *Didelphis virginiana* has an efficient pouch.

6

The oldest marsupial remains, or *fossils*, have been found in North America. They date back 130 million years to the *Cretaceous period*. Until recently scientists believed that the opossum was a *living fossil*, an animal that has not changed in millions of years. But it is not. The earliest known remains of the Virginia opossum date from the *Pleistocene epoch*. That epoch began only a million years ago. During that time, glaciers covered about one-fourth of the earth. It is also known as the Ice Age.

About 65 *species* of opossums live in Mexico and Central and South America. The Virginia opossum is the only marsupial that lives in North America. Its range extends southward to Costa Rica in Central America.

The marsupials that abound in Australia and New Guinea include many animals called possums. They live mostly in trees. They are not related to the Virginia opossum.

An animal with many names

Captain John Smith gave the strange creature he had never seen in his native England the name Virginia opossum. The Virginia part came about because that was the name of the area Captain Smith was colonizing. He didn't know the animal lived in places other than Virginia.

Some people insist that the "o" in front of "possum"

was a mistake. One story is that Captain Smith made the error because he didn't hear correctly. He asked a Powhatan the animal's name. Surprised at the white man's ignorance, the Powhatan said, "Oh. Possum." Captain Smith misunderstood and gave the marsupial an Irish-sounding name.

Native Americans called it by many names. The Cherokees called it *seequa*. The Choctaws called it *shookhuta*. And the Tuscaroras' name was *cheera*. The Mayans called it *och*, and to the Aztecs it was *tlaquatzin*. The present Mexican name, *tlacuache*, is similar to the ancient Aztec name. But the official name—the one scientists use—is *opossum*. It is derived from the Algonquian word *apasum*, which means "white animal."

Describing an opossum

People who had never seen an opossum before they came to America described it in letters to relatives in their native countries as being "the size of a small dog with the face of a fox and the ears of a bat." Colonist Richard Eden didn't have a name for it, but there is no doubt that he was describing the opossum when he wrote in 1555 about a beast "with a snowte lyke a foxe, a tayle lyke a marmasette, eares lyke a batte, handes lyke a man, and feete lyke an ape." Captain Smith wrote, "An Opassum

Early colonists described the common opossum as having the characteristics of a fox, bat, pig, rat, cat, and ape.

hath an head like a Swine, and a taile like a Rat, and is of the bignes of a Cat."

Opossums grow from two feet to almost three feet long. Their tails are between ten and thirteen inches long.

Like most furred animals, they have two layers of fur. The outer layer is made up of coarse guard hairs. The underfur is softer and finer than the guard hairs. The guard hairs are generally grayish white. The underfur is generally white tipped with black. Some opossums are nearly black, and a few are brown. Young opossums are darker than full-grown opossums.

The opossum has a white, or yellow-white, head. The *vibrissa*, or whiskers, scattered around its face look like long, thin spikes. It has a long snout and a pink nose. The naked ears are gray. The opossum's large pupils help it see well at night. They make the eyes look like black beads.

Guard hair grows out over the base of the tail. Except for a few scattered hairs, the rest of the tail is bare. The top third of it is dark and scaly. The lower part is yellowish-white or pink.

The tail is *prehensile*, which means grasping. Opossums can grasp objects with their tails, but pictures of them hanging by their tails are inaccurate. Opossums do not naturally hang by their tails. Photographers and artists have put the animals in that position. If an opossum is stealing eggs from a bird's nest on a tree limb, it may wrap its tail around the limb above for extra security. But the tail is not a "fifth hand," as it is sometimes described.

An opossum's tail is, however, important to its well-being. The tip curves down and touches the ground or the tree the opossum is climbing. It seems to be a sensor. It may even help to warn that a *predator* is approaching. The position of an opossum's tail is a good indicator of its health. A healthy opossum walks with its tail low and the tip down. A sick one curls its tail upward.

An opossum's front feet have five toes, each with a claw. The back feet have five toes also, but only four toes have claws. The big toe, or thumb, has a nail and is *opposable*, like a person's thumb. Since the thumb can curve

An opossum's back feet have five toes, but only four of the toes have claws.

inward, the back feet are an asset when the opossum climbs a tree.

The opossum has strong smelling and hearing senses. Its jaws are strong. It has 50 teeth—more than any other American land *mammal*. It grunts, hisses, growls, and whines. During mating, it makes a clicking sound with its teeth. Young opossums cry when they are separated from their mothers.

Like all marsupials, the opossum has a small brain. A raccoon's skull is about the same size as an opossum's, but its brain is seven times as large.

Perhaps to make up for their small brains, opossums are remarkably adaptable. They have managed to survive in a world where smarter animals have become *extinct*.

CHAPTER TWO:

Suppose two people who knew nothing about opossums were assigned to study them. One person was to watch them at night. The other was to study them during the day. The reports would be so different they would seem to describe two totally different animals.

The opossum at night

Whether they live in a state like Florida with a subtropical climate, or in cold northern Minnesota, opossums are *nocturnal*. At night, they are fast and elusive. When they are trying to escape from a predator, they can climb a tree with ease. They also like to run into openings at the bottoms of hollow tree trunks. They quickly climb upward—out of sight and out of reach.

If an opossum is cornered at night, it will hiss and show all 50 of its teeth. It looks so terrifying that many a predator has had second thoughts about attacking. If the enemy is no larger than the opossum, the opossum will fight. It stares at the other animal with its black eyes. It grabs the challenger in its strong jaws and shakes it vigorously in a figure eight.

The common opossum never picks a fight with another animal. It only fights if it absolutely has to.

A daytime death act

By day, opossums mostly sleep. If they leave their dens, they are sluggish and docile. Because they don't have their wits about them, it is easy for predators to surprise them. They may at first make a show of fighting back, but their chief daytime defense is to fall into a *comatose* state called "playing possum." That is, they go into a trancelike state that makes predators think they are dead. Not all opossums do this. An opossum can stay in this state from a few minutes up to several hours. It works well. An animal that is already dead doesn't interest most predators.

The death act is very convincing. The opossum goes limp and lies curled up on its side. Its mouth hangs open and its tongue lolls out. Its eyes are open. Its breathing is so slow and shallow it cannot be detected. The opossum

To protect itself from predators during the day, an opossum can fall into a comatose state, which makes the predators think the opossum is dead.

does not react to prodding, shaking, or even to severe pain.

Some observers believe an opossum makes itself go into this comatose state. They have done brain wave tests on opossums that are in the trance. The tests show that the animal is fully alert. Since it is alert, these people argue, it must be using a special talent to put on a superb act.

Other people think opossums cannot control this behavior. They say the tests do not prove that opossums put themselves in the trance voluntarily. Some people, they point out, freeze in dangerous situations. It is not intentional, and the people are aware of what is happening around them.

Whether it is a purposely *feigned* death, or an uncontrollable reaction, that particular gift has saved many opossums from becoming a predator's meal.

CHAPTER THREE:

Opossums need very little—food, water, and a place to build their nests. They aren't picky about their nesting spots or their food, but they like to live near streams or ponds. Opossums not only need water to drink. They also love to wade and swim.

Almost any place will do

A hollow stump, a pile of junk, a space beneath an old barn—almost any place will do for a nesting site. On open land, an opossum may nest in a brush stack. In a rocky area, it finds a safe crevice. In a town, it might choose a culvert or a hedge. A hollow tree in a front yard where there are no dogs makes a good home. Sometimes an opossum lives under a house while its occupants walk on the floor right above it. It might even move into a basement where there is little traffic.

Opossums choose homes that will protect them from their enemies. Hollow trees make ideal homes for opossum families.

It does not bother opossums at all to move into another animal's home. They have been known to settle down in vacated woodchuck *burrows* and nests left empty by squirrels. They gather grass and leaves to make the used nests more comfortable. Corn shucks are also useful to opossums renovating nests.

An opossum's tail comes in handy when it is nest-making time. An opossum picks up dry leaves with its mouth, then takes the leaves from its mouth with its front feet. The front feet pass the leaves to the back feet, which send them on to the tail. The tail makes a loop and serves as a basket. The leaf gathering is a quick, smooth procedure.

Opossums do not have a fixed *home range* like many other animals. The home range is the area over which an animal searches for food. The area varies according to the animal. A coyote, for example, has a home range of about 30 miles. A rabbit's home range is much smaller— about five miles.

A male opossum's home range is around the den he is sleeping in. He may cover a mile in either direction, or five miles, depending on the availability of food. The next week he may move to the other side of a lake and check out the food over there. When the female opossum isn't expecting or taking care of young, her range changes as much as the male's range.

A nesting opossum mother doesn't move to another place unless she has to move. She *forages* only as far as she needs to in order to find food.

Opossums are not territorial like most other animals.

An opossum may travel up to five miles away from its den in search of food.

An animal's *territory* is the yard space around its den. A coyote will fight another coyote to defend its territory. An opossum won't. It won't even fight over its den. If it comes home after a night of searching for food and finds another opossum in its den, it takes one of two courses. It leaves and finds a vacant den, or it climbs in beside the stranger and goes to sleep.

Female opossums sometimes share a den. So do male opossums. But males and females never share the same sleeping quarters.

Even when opossums share dens, they are basically loners. They put up with each other while they are resting during the day. But when they leave in the evening to forage, they go separate ways.

A favorite pastime

An opossum may spend a long time just wading in the water. But if it is in the mood to swim, it doesn't just paddle. It swims well and uses a variety of strokes. It dives. It swims underwater. Some people say they have heard opossums make contented, purring sounds while they are swimming. There are also times when water represents safety. In the woods, an opossum doesn't stand a chance against a wildcat. If it can reach water, it may escape.

What opossums eat

The main part of an opossum's diet is meat. That includes fresh meat, meat that has begun to spoil, and rotten meat. A frog cannot hop fast enough to escape a hungry opossum. A crayfish makes a crunchy snack. An opossum slurps up earthworms and is particularly fond of beetles. But a bird that's been dead a couple of days is fine, too. So is a dead deer. And to an opossum, finding a loose sack of garbage is like finding a gold mine.

The opossum is a good swimmer. It uses a number of different strokes and can dive underwater.

Opossums also eat vegetables. Dried corn is a favorite dish. They like berries and apples. When persimmons (fruits about the size of large plums) ripen in the fall, opossums are delighted. When they eat persimmons, opossums spit out the seeds.

After dining, opossums clean themselves carefully. In fact, the notion that opossums are dirty animals is entirely wrong. They like to take baths in streams or ponds. They spend a lot of time washing their fur with their tongues. They are particularly finicky about their tails.

While opossums have a big appetite any time of the year, fall is a time for gorging. They eat ravenously and put on a thick layer of fat. This is especially important for opossums that live in areas where winters are long and cold.

Cold weather takes a toll

Opossums used to live in areas of America where winters are not harsh. But they roamed far and were introduced to other areas by people who wanted to see if opossums could adapt to drier or colder climates. Their range has greatly expanded. Opossums now live in dry western states. They also live in areas where winter temperatures are often below freezing, or even below zero. They have to contend with biting wind and deep snow.

In the fall, an opossum's favorite food is a ripe persimmon.

In the winter, when food is scarce, an opossum may not search for food and water for several days at a time.

24

Because they spend so much time in their dens, opossums seem to *hibernate* in the winter, but they don't. True hibernators, like ground squirrels, are hard to awaken. Opossums may stay in their dens and sleep a lot for several days, but they go out when they get hungry. If the ground is covered with deep snow, it is hard to find enough food to keep from starving. Even in areas where it does not snow, the winter landscape is apt to be bare.

If the opossum finds enough food to survive, it may still be harmed by extreme cold weather. The naked ears and the bare, pink portion of the tail may get frostbitten. Severe frostbite causes *gangrene*, which destroys body tissue. It is not uncommon to see an opossum in winter with the pink part of its tail gone. And since its tail is so important to it, an opossum that loses its tail may languish and die.

CHAPTER FOUR:

During the breeding season, female opossums are in *heat*, or able to get pregnant, an average of every 29 days. In warm climates, breeding begins as early as December. In cooler areas, it begins in January. In cold climates it does not start until February.

Breeding season extends through spring and summer into autumn. Opossums generally have two *litters* a year. In some southern states, they may have three.

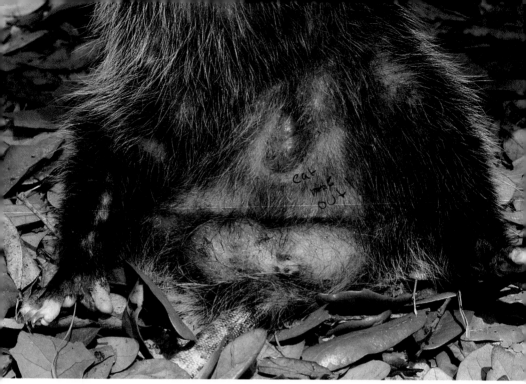

Newborn opossums are barely visible inside the mother's pouch.

After mating, the male opossum goes on his way. For the female, a long ordeal has just begun.

A pouch full of young

A female opossum has 20 to 25 eggs. But she has no more than 13 *teats*, or nipples. Newborns must latch on to a nipple to survive. Fortunately, all the eggs are not likely to be fertilized during mating.

On the thirteenth day after mating, the young opossums are born. When the mother goes into labor, she stands on her hind legs in a bent position. She licks her pouch and her nipples clean. Even after the teats are clean, she keeps licking them, probably because they are tender and sore.

The newborn is about the size of a corn kernel. It weighs seven-hundredths of an ounce and looks like a pink blob with a frog's face. Skin tissue covers its eyes. Its mouth is wide and the face muscles are strong because it must suck constantly to survive. Its back legs are only stumps, but its front legs and feet are formed. Its front feet have temporary claws to help it reach the pouch.

As each tiny opossum is born, the mother licks off the

A close-up view of a female's pouch shows its young, which are each about the size of a kernel of corn.

fluid that surrounds it. Otherwise it would smother. She also licks the fur from her *vulva* to her pouch. This marks the road for the infant to follow in its hand-over-hand upward climb of about three inches. If it bumps into dry hair, it immediately veers back onto the damp path that will lead it to the pouch.

Strong newborns make it to the pouch in about a minute. Weaker ones take longer. Only about 60 percent make it at all. Once the infant reaches the pouch, it must search through a forest of hair for a nipple no bigger than a pin head. When the baby finds a nipple, it latches on and doesn't let go for two months.

If a newborn reaches the pouch and all the teats are taken, it dies. Those that do find a nipple change rapidly. Within a few days, the claws they used to climb to the pouch fall off. Inside that crowded space, claws would make life miserable, both for the mother and the newborns. Each blind little infant begins to develop and take the shape of an opossum.

Some wrong notions

In the past, people who studied the opossum made various wrong assumptions about the newborn and the teat it attaches itself to. They saw the mother poke her nose into her pouch. (She was licking her pouch and nipples.) They

Once the newborn has reached its mother's pouch, it attaches itself to one of her nipples. The newborn will stay there for two months.

didn't see the tiny creatures making their way up to the pouch. But suddenly, there they were. These people concluded that the mother had sneezed them into the pouch.

Less than 30 years ago, some articles and books made other errors. They said the infant swallowed the nipple. They also said the mother pumped the milk into the young's stomach. There's a good reason these wrong assumptions were made. The young are inside a crowded, furry pouch. That pouch has to be full of carbon dioxide. Opossum students wondered how the young could get enough oxygen to have the energy to suck. But they do. And those who study opossums now think the warm, stale air helps the young.

A patient mother

At first, the mother opossum continues to enjoy climbing trees. She closes her pouch tight so no water can get into it and goes for a swim. When the babies become heavy, she doesn't climb, swim, or dive as much. Even walking is tedious. But she must search diligently for food or she will not have enough milk for her hungry, growing young.

At nine weeks, the young opossums' eyes open, and they start coming out of the pouch for brief periods. They climb all over their mother. The bold ones may even venture a short distance away from her. But they are not yet able to control their own body temperatures. They can't stay out of the pouch for long.

As the days pass, the young leave the nipples for longer and longer intervals. They still scamper back to the pouch at the slightest sign of danger. And they still suck and suck. If it is a hot day, the mother relaxes her pouch. The young climb outside it without letting go of the teats. By this time the nipples have stretched enough to accommodate such long-distance nursing.

On a hot day, a female's young can continue to nurse after climbing out of the pouch.

A female opossum carries her eight-week-old young as she climbs onto a tree stump.

The hazards of growing up

By the time they are 11 weeks old, the young opossums spend a good deal of time outside the pouch. They learn to find beetles and other food. When the mother takes a stroll or climbs a tree, they ride on her back.

Perhaps you have seen photographs of baby opossums on their mother's back with their tails wrapped around hers. These photos are posed. Young opossums wrap their tails around their mother's tail only when the mother is running for safety.

When the young are on her back, a mother opossum does not play dead to defend herself. Her offspring would surely be gobbled up. She takes flight. She throws her tail over her back. The little ones dig their claws into her fur and wrap their tails around hers. They hang on. If one falls off, or is knocked off when she runs through brush, the mother must leave it.

When they are about three months old, the young opossums are *weaned* and become self-reliant. In captivity, 50 percent or more of the original litter may make it to that point. In the wild, where survival of the fittest is the rule, only about 25 percent of the litter are still alive.

After three months, a young opossum is weaned and can explore its habitats on its own.

By adulthood, an opossum weighs 28,000 times its weight at birth. That's hard for people to imagine. On an average, adult humans weigh only 20 times their birth weights.

CHAPTER FIVE:

The small percentage of opossums that make it to adulthood in their natural environment find life hard. Beset by many dangers, they have a life span of about two years.

Diseases and parasites

Intestinal *parasites* infect opossums because their diet includes *carrion* and other garbage. They may have tapeworms and roundworms in their alimentary tracts. *Flukes* invade their lungs. Fleas take up residence in their long hair. Ticks sap their strength and cause infections.

Because an opossum's diet includes garbage, it is sometimes in danger of carrying parasites.

The opossum as prey

Opossums are natural *prey* for coyotes and wildcats. But dogs are their worst enemies. An opossum may put on a death act to prevent the dog from killing it, but it may later die anyway. A violent shaking or mauling is apt to break or dislocate some of the opossum's bones. Left crippled and weakened, it is a ready target for disease.

There was a time when steel traps closed around many opossums' legs. Their pelts were used to make fur coats, or for fur trim on cloth coats. Sometimes the fur was dyed to look like another animal's fur. Opossum fur is not durable, though. There are still trapping seasons, but getting caught in a trap is not the danger it once was.

Today, highways are the worst hazard for opossums. In their night foraging, they start across a highway. A car or truck's bright lights bear down on them. They may freeze, or they may run. Either way, they are likely to be killed.

Opossum hunting is a sport in some areas. It isn't difficult to train a dog to tree an opossum at night. The hunter then shines a flashlight on the opossum. Sometimes the hunter shoots it. Sometimes it is shaken down from the tree and taken alive.

Each year, forest fires kill thousands of opossums. Trees in the opossums' natural *habitat* are destroyed for

A hunter trains his dog to keep an opossum trapped in a tree.

paper and other products. Development projects, during which stores and houses are built on fields and former forests, destroy the opossums' dens and foraging areas.

Modern farming methods also make survival difficult for opossums. The patches of woods farmers used to leave standing on their land are gone. Haystacks where opossums had cozy winter homes are gone, too.

In captivity

It is not difficult to raise opossums. They even get used to having people around. If one manages to get through the fencing, however, don't expect it to come back. An opossum will let you pick it up and stroke it, but it will be nervous and fidgety. And you can't teach an opossum to play a game, not even a simple one like fetch. About the most interesting thing an opossum in captivity ever does is wake up and eat.

An opossum in captivity does not lose its natural *instincts*. When it senses that it is time to build a nest, it will tear up newspapers and place the shreds in its tail-loop basket. Then, since it already has a perfectly good nest, it will wander aimlessly.

For the opossum, there is a good side to the easy life of captivity. It lives longer. Some owners say an opossum can survive in captivity for as long as seven years.

An opossum kept in captivity will get used to people, although it will not lose its natural instincts.

Eating opossum

The Cherokees would not eat opossum. The meat, they said, was unclean. But people rich and poor do eat opossum. Cooks use various methods of scrubbing or soaking it before baking.

Some opossum cooks advise that an opossum should be kept in a cage for two weeks before it is slaughtered. During that time, they say, it should be fed only buttermilk and corn. Sweet potatoes go well with opossum, which tastes something like pork.

CHAPTER SIX:

The Virginia opossum that lives in Mexico and Central America has many marsupial cousins. More relatives live in South America. And they come in all shapes and sizes. The tiny *Monodelphis* looks like a shrew. The *Marmosa* look like mice. The thick-tail (*Lutreolina*) and the yapok (*Chironestes*) grow to be two feet long, from nose to tail.

Mouse opossums, yapoks, and others

From Northern Mexico to Argentina, there are 40 species of *Marmosa*—mouse or murine opossums. Mouse opossums lack pouches. Folds of skin protect the nipples and the newborns.

The yapok, or yapock, is also called the yapo or water opossum. It is found from Honduras and El Salvador in Central America to Paraguay in South America. The tail accounts for more than half of its length.

The yapok has a delicate face and big eyes. Its ears look like round fans. The short, soft fur is silver-gray and black—like light and dark shadows. A semiaquatic opossum, it has webbed back feet and depends on fresh water for its food. It catches small fish, crustaceans, and aquatic insects. It stores the catch in its cheek pouches until it is lazing on the water's surface or on the bank.

The yapok fishes at night. During the day, it sleeps in a hole in a bank just above water level. When it does not have a good hole, it may temporarily sleep on the ground in a nest of leaves.

Of all opossums, the yapok has the best pouch, and its four to six young are born perfectly formed. They are not

The brown four-eyed opossum has two white patches over its eyes, which make it look as if it has four eyes.

yet strong, though, and stay in the pouch for several weeks. The mother yapok closes her fur-lined pouch water-tight while she fishes.

The *Monodelphis* lives in the Amazon forests. It is only three inches long. The thick-tailed opossum lives in southern Brazil. A short-legged animal, it resembles a weasel and is fiercely *carnivorous*.

Two species of woolly opossums (*Caluromys*) live in the northern Andes.

The gray four-eyed opossum (*Philandes*) and the brown four-eyed opossum (*Metachirus nudicaudatus*) of Central and South America are the size of rats. Large white spots over their eyes give them the appearance of having four eyes. Instead of pouches, the brown four-eyed female has folds of skin on either side of the nipples.

The *Monodelphis domestica* is popular with Brazilian homemakers. It kills insects and rodents in the dwellings where it lives.

The opossum's future

When you consider what has happened to its natural habitat, from the loss of forests to the loss of farmland haystacks, the future of opossums would seem doubtful. And yet, they have fared better than the wildcat and other animals that are much more intelligent.

Just in this century, their range has expanded hundreds of miles northward. They go as far north as Ontario and British Columbia. Since being introduced by people to California, they now live all along the west coast. A small population lives in New Mexico. Opossums have spread into eastern Colorado from Kansas and into Wyoming from Nebraska.

Like all wild animals, the peaceful, humble opossum faces many dangers in the modern world. Will it survive? Or will it become extinct?

There are factors in its favor. It is not particularly exciting to hunt. It can tolerate human beings and their habits. It has an excellent defense against four-legged predators. And it is not a picky eater. It seems safe to assume that the opossum will be around far into the future.

GLOSSARY/INDEX:

46

INDEX/GLOSSARY: